7 KEYS

FOR A PROPHETIC LIFE

PHILLIP BRYANT

ISBN: 979-8-218-27161-9

ISBN: 979-8-218-27162-6

Book Design by HMDpublishing

DEDICATIONS

I dedicate this book to my beautiful mother, Dr. Gloriet Jean Laster Boyd. She was more than a mom, she was my friend, pastor, and inspiration. In life, I had not many people that I wanted to be like when I grew up, but I had Glo Jean. She embodied love, mercy, forgiveness, and unwavering devotion to Jesus. My mom would testify about when she received Christ and left her old life how she never looked back! I think of how she led a life of honor before me all my life. She taught me everything I know about love, relationships, life, forgiveness, and expectations. I wish that she was here to read this, but I know that she's in the presence of the Lord enjoying her reward now. Mom, I did it. You were the first author in our family. Because of your exemplary leadership, I was able to write this book. I love you immensely and I can't wait to see you in Heaven one day.

I dedicate this book to my beautiful wife, Hope Bryant. This book would not have been completed had it not been for you. The way you believe in me is scary at times, I honestly am blown away by the confidence you have in me. You have given me language and added color to my life. Being your husband is one of the greatest joys that God has given me. Thank you for loving me, listening to my random thoughts, and remembering them when I share them repeatedly. You told me when we were dating that you'd follow me wherever I go, and you have not abandoned that word yet. Thank you,

Hope. You mean the world to me. Thank you for being my friend, lover, and cheerleader. I am because of you.

I dedicate this book to my spiritual father, Prophet Dale Pace. I could write an entire book on you, Pop. You came into my life for so many reasons, but the most important was to be a father to me. I appreciate every lesson, phone call, lunch, prophetic word, and time spent together over the years. You called me a prophet while I was amid an identity crisis. I didn't know who I was, but you saw what God placed in my life. You encouraged me daily and have given me opportunities to grow and express who I am in the earth. This book would not be if I had not met you. God bless the day that Dale Pace, Sr. was born. This book goes to you, young man. I love you and thank you for your impartation and example to be a disciple for Jesus.

Lastly, I dedicate this book to you. Your support in my ministry has fueled me for the journey. Thank you for following me as I follow Christ and believing in the words the Lord has given me to share with the world. It is my hope that you are strengthened, encouraged, and aligned with the will of God concerning your life. I desire to see you develop a healthy supernatural experience with God that many people will be blessed by. I appreciate you.

Lord, create in me a clean heart. Thank you, that you desire to dwell with me, speak to me and speak through me. I ask that you be glorified, and your people be strengthened and edified as we search the Scriptures to come into revelation about what you want us to know. Thank you. Amen.

CONTENTS

INTRODUCTION

WHAT ARE KEYS?

If there is one thing to know about me, it is that I love words. I love understanding their meaning and the revelation God often gives me as I study. So, when I began to write this book I first asked, "What are keys?" Outside of the obvious technical definition I saw, the thing that stuck with me the most is that keys are given to people for access. When my wife and I purchased our home there were several steps we had to go through before we were given our key. The key was a transfer of power, the transfer of access. It was the final thing saying we were the owner and have complete authority over the place we bought.

I believe that it's important to start this conversation about keys for a prophetic life simply stating that we have been giving delegated authority and premier access to the presence of God. Romans 12:3 tells us God has given to each man a measure of faith. Metron is the Greek word found in that scripture and means a determined extent, portion measured, or in other words, a sphere of influence, authority, and anointing.

So based upon our measure of faith we have been given authority which gives us access, a key, to the presence of God. Now this access only works through a relationship with the Holy Spirit so before we talk about the keys, tools, and strategies to strengthen your prophetic journey we must stop and make a point about knowing Holy Spirit. It is impossible for us to have keys and access to the presence of God without having a relationship with God. We come to know God through our relationship with the Holy Spirit. The first thing to know is that the Holy Spirit is the key. I want to say that again: Holy Spirit is the key! How we utilize and prioritize our time of worship and communion with the Holy Spirit readies and prepare us to have access to the mind of God in a personal and revelatory way.

WHAT IS A PROPHETIC LIFE?

A prophetic life is a life that eagerly expects the word of the Lord. Matthew 4:4 tells us that man should not live by bread alone, but by every word that proceeds out of the mouth of God. Living a prophetic life simply means that every day I posture myself in eager expectation for the word of God. It is the word of God that not only shapes my day, but my perspective, my expectations, my hopes, my dreams, my desires, my outcomes, and my personality. Hebrews 11:3 says that by His Word were the worlds framed. A prophetic life that is framed by the Word of God does not move, plan, buy, consider, make an agreement without first consulting Holy Spirit. A prophetic life isn't marked nor is it shaped by one's own opinions, but it must be shaped by the word of God. Proverbs 3:4-5 tells us to trust in the Lord with all our heart and lean not to our own understanding but acknowledge Him in all our ways and He will direct our path. To walk in a prophetic life, you must fully lean on and trust in God which often means to abandon your own counsel and thoughts about what your life should look like. Romans 8:14 tells us that whoever is led by the Spirit of God are considered sons of God.

The purpose of a prophetic life is to have and produce love, joy, peace, patience, kindness, goodness, faithfulness, gentleness, and self-control. Sound familiar? It is the fruit of the Spirit being expressed through a person, along with the gifts of the Spirit, that matters most.

It is imperative that we not only do, but BE. Hebrews 11:6 tells us that anyone that comes to God must first believe that He EXISTS, and that He is a rewarder of them that diligently seek Him. God is so concerned about us knowing our identity, and not operating out of a false narrative of having to work to be rewarded.

Romans 8 shows us that as sons and daughters of God, through the adoption of Jesus Christ, we can freely walk after the law of the Spirit and reap the benefits as Kingdom joint-heirs with Christ Jesus. We can live a prophetic life!

As believers in Jesus Christ, we have been granted this amazing opportunity to live a prophetic life. The blood of Jesus was sufficient payment for our sins, and because He gave His life for us, we are now made free from the power of sin and death. As prophetic people, we must always look unto Jesus because without his atonement we would not have access to the Father. Through his selfless act of pure devotion and love, we are made to know Him through a personal relationship with Holy Spirit.

How do you live a prophetic life, you ask? You must be willing to choose to abandon your own way, life, and thoughts to pick up your cross and follow Jesus. A prophetic life is a life that is madly in love with Jesus, and at all costs will follow Him unashamedly.

KEY

A PURE HEART

A lot of teaching on the prophetic focuses on being precise and accurate but there is not enough focus on seeing God. Those things matter but often distract us from what's most important. So, what happens when we do not have a pure heart before the Lord? We aren't allowed access to see God.

> **Psalm 24:3-4**
> *Who can ascend the hill of the Lord? Who can stand in his holy sanctuary?*
> *Only the one with clean hands and a pure heart; the one who hasn't made false promises, the one who hasn't sworn dishonestly.*

Being pure in heart is not having ill motives toward people and towards God. It's not being full of pride and trying to be prophetically accurate for self-gain.

It's not being nosey or using the gifts of God to manipulate, tamper, and clamor for attention.

The Lord in his sovereignty is not going to let any of us share or steal his glory! If our motives are right, our intentions are pure, and our desires are to seek the Lord while he may be found, we will be able to come into a level of accuracy to be able to see God. Hebrew 11:6 reminds us that whoever wants access to God must first believe that He is and that he is a rewarder of them that diligently seek him.

So, to live a prophetic life is to perfect your seek, perfect your pursuit!

You can't pursue after a holy God with impure motives. You won't find him! But when you open your heart to be purified you can receive all of the Father in his glory and splendor. When our hearts are right and our intentions are pure, there is a holy place we can reach in our relationship with God, in worship, in prayer, in obedience, in giving, in serving. He summons us up to a higher place, a deeper place!

We come from the outer courts to the inner courts to the holy of holies!

In this place we stand, and we see him as Hakadosh: holy, powerful, and fully deserving of all worship and adoration. Seeing God as Hakadosh causes our spirit and our flesh to allow him to perfect our ability to see him and the way that we believe in him!

> **Matthew 5:8**
> *Blessed are the pure in heart, for they shall see God.*

You shall see God!

This scripture is not just talking about the end of this life only, but this is a prophetic key given to us by the spirit of God that through our relationship we have access to see him as he is. The reason why many of us struggle to see God and live a prophetic life through that sight, it is because we don't act have an accurate view of who it is we say we believe in!

So, when you hear that phrase "you shall see God" it's about an experience, an encounter, an impact. When you have an experience for yourself, it's about what you felt, what you heard, what that experience meant. It's written on your psyche, your heart. If you take a moment to pause and reflect, your body even remembers what it felt like when you first saw God and received his love.

I bet you're wondering why I am harping so much on seeing God.

2 Corinthians 3: 18
So, all of us who have had that veil removed can see and reflect the glory of the Lord. And the Lord—who is the Spirit—makes us more and more like him as we are changed into his glorious image.

You see Him. You become like Him.

Say it loud: I see Him!

Isaiah 6:3 says holy, holy, holy is the Lord God almighty; the whole earth is full of his glory! Because the whole earth is full of Him, we can see and identify him in the earth. We can see him in different cultures. We can see him in society. We can see him in the lives of people. We can see him in business and in government. We can see his desires for parents and family. We can see him in the educational system. We can see him in the entertainment and the judicial system. We can see Him everywhere.

The Lord is truly concerned about what is within the heart of men and women. Proverbs 23:7 tells us that as a man thinks in his heart, so is he. What is held in your heart impacts your entire life! One of the biggest road-blocks of living a prophetic life is not having a pure heart.

It requires that you are honest with yourself about your intentions, motives, desires, and devotion. Do you truly set God above everything that you love? Are you desiring to use your prophetic intel to your advantage to gain the applause of men?

It is imperative that we pray for the Lord to give us a pure heart. How we experience life shapes our perspective and impacts our beliefs. If we are not careful to remain both prayerful and accountable to the Holy Spirit and a spirit-led community, we could allow the issues we encounter in life to cause our hearts to grow cold, calloused, bitter, hateful, and contentious. Proverbs 4:23 tells us to keep our heart with all vigilance, for from it flow the springs of life.

When we "keep" our hearts it takes investigation, intention, and immediate action on our part to guard what comes in and out of our hearts. We are required to do something! One of the ways that you guard, or keep, your heart is to make sure you have on the full armor of God. The breastplate of righteousness and the shield of faith help to defend, deflect, and protect us from the attacks that will come at our hearts.

Although life will impact us, and seemingly find ways to creep under our armor and pierce us in the heart, God is a healer! Psalm 34:18 declares that God is near to those who are of a broken heart and saves those who are crushed in spirit.

It's easy to overlook and move past nagging things that are secretly being deposited into our hearts. We must be vigilant as believers to evaluate and examine our hearts daily so that Jesus can express himself purely to us and through us.

2

I'VE GOT AN INNER WITNESS

've always been bold in my faith, especially when I became aware of the prophetic gift on my life. There would be times when I would be in prophetic activations, or even prophetic moments in service where I would always jump to go first. There was this unspoken confidence that I had in my spirit that when it's time to prophesy, I can do it without prompting. As I've been cultivating my prophetic life with the Lord, He spoke to me through his word regarding an "inner witness."

Holy Spirit, the Spirit of God, is our inner witness. He leads us into all truth. The Spirit of God, also known as the Spirit of truth, leads and guides the children of God daily. Not only is the Holy Spirit our inner witness, but he is the true witness of both the Father and the Son.

A witness is defined as any person having knowledge of truth willing to testify to that truth.

> **Romans 8:16**
> *The Spirit himself bears witness with our spirit that we are sons of God.*

The Holy Spirit which we received from God through salvation, gave us the ability to call him, "Abba Father'. Romans 8:15 tells us that the spirit that we received was not of slavery or bondage, but adoption. In this exchange that we experience as believers, our spirit has been given a comforter that reminds us of who we are to God.

It's so important for believers to be filled with the Holy Spirit because he testifies to the knowledge and truth concerning who Jesus is to us, and who we are to Jesus! The Holy Spirit testifies to us of who God the Father is as well. We come into a deeper fellowship with Jesus Christ as we fellowship with our witness, the spirit of truth.

The confidence I have in my prophetic life is rooted in my fellowship with the Spirit of God that literally lives in my body. The scriptures reveal that we are temples of the Holy Spirit, a place that the Spirit himself dwells on the inside of us. When I forget who I am on my journey, my inner witness, my comforter, reminds me that I am a son of God. Through this continual exchange between my spirit and The Spirit himself, I grow stronger in my faith, love, and devotion towards God.

In building a prophetic life, you will need to be well acquainted with the Holy Spirit as your inner witness. My caution to you is do not allow other witnesses to speak over Holy Spirit. Fear, failure, hopelessness, sin, condemnation, anger, bitterness, rage, envy, low self-esteem, and a few others are vying for the Speaker of the House seat in your life. Don't allow them! Holy Spirit is the pure spirit of God that comes to aid you in your journey to be more like Jesus, and to be an effective witness for Him.

Here's the truth, we have been given the Holy Spirit to give us the advantage in the Earth. Does having an inner witness who is perfectly connected to God make us better than anyone else? Absolutely not! It does offer us privileges that are only given to citizens of the Kingdom of God. Our inner witness will speak to us about past, current, and future things which is why being a good steward of what you receive is of utmost importance. Write down what your inner witness tells you in dreams, visions, or through prophetic utterance. What good is having information without knowing how to apply it?

> ### John 16:13
> *But when He, the Spirit of Truth comes, He will guide you into all the Truth. For He will not speak His own message or on His own authority]; but He will tell whatever He hears from the Father; He will give the message that has been given to Him, and He will announce and declare to you the things that are to come.*

The Holy Spirit, our inner witness, literally embodies the whole truth, and still leads us into all truth. Our flesh fights us in hosting the Holy Spirit because truth brings conviction, and the bible tells us that the flesh hates God. The Holy Ghost develops us into people who live by truth, walk by truth, and speak by truth.

> ### Psalm 51:6
> *Behold, you desire truth in the inward parts, and in the hidden part You will make me to know wisdom. Purge me with hyssop, and I shall be clean; Wash me, and I shall be whiter than snow.*

We will have times in our lives, as I have had plenty, where we need the Lord to cleanse us on the inside. Truth being planted in our soul manifests wisdom in our decisions. We are purged through the truth that the Holy Spirit brings to us.

As we continue to cultivate an ear to hear truth for our lives, we experience Holy Spirit speaking to us about humanity and the world around us. Your inner witness has something to say to everyone. Let me say it like this, God wants to chat with everyone He created. As a believer, you now become the vessel, who has been purified by truth and the blood of Jesus, that God will speak through. This is how we as New Covenant believers' prophesy: the Holy Spirit tells us whatever He hears from the Father by announcing the message to us in dreams, visions, prayer, or our time of worship. We then communicate the message with the person, group, community, or nation through the prophetic expressions and streams that the Holy Spirit placed within us. Some will sing the prophetic word, dance it out, draw or paint it out, play it out musically through instruments, write it out as a scribe, while some will prophesy verbally through words. Our inner witness declares the message from The Father to bring edification, exhortation, and comfort to a person. This should be the fruit of a prophetic word inspired by the Holy Ghost.

Our prophetic life is shaped entirely by the inspiration, leadership, and authority of the Holy Spirit because He leads us into all truth. Following His lead aligns us with the word of God which connects our inner witness to being sons of God. As you journey through building a prophetic life that postures itself in obedience and truth, you will grow a stronger bond with your inner witness.

We have an inner witness that has the inside scoop on everything that God wants the entire world to know. Use your prophetic key to engage with Him, spend time with Him, develop a relationship with your inner witness so that you can walk in the law of the spirit, and build the prophetic life the bible tells us expressly that we can have.

I declare that as you utilize this prophetic key, developing a relationship with the Holy Spirit, that you will grow in a boldness, confidence, and trust that is un-shakeable. You can do all that God has called you to, build what He instructed you to, and accomplish every task He's placed upon your life by partnering with your inner witness. Your inner witness knows the mind of Christ, and with that intel, He knows you also. Let Holy Spirit help you, guide you, lead you, instruct you in the ways of the Lord, as you continue to grow and develop.

KEY

3

WORSHIP IS OBEDIENCE

Worship is a critical key to forming a prophetic life. When we look at the word worship, it's defined as the feeling or expression of reverence and adoration for a deity. As I've studied the scriptures, I have learned that worship is not one-dimensional. When we worship God, we acknowledge, praise, and thank Him for who He is and what He's done. We express our honor to, revere, and adore Him. Worshipping God is the reason we were created! We were designed to be His glory in the earth so that the works of our hands would worship Him.

Worship has so many beautiful forms from singing and crying to thanksgiving and confession. As beautiful as all those things are, worship is so much more! It is how we posture ourselves before Him daily. Worship brings our mind, body, soul, and spirit into alignment with the will of the Lord, and Holy Spirit.

> **Deuteronomy 30:6**
> *The Lord your God will circumcise your hearts and the hearts of your descendants, so that you may love him with all your heart and with all your soul, and live.*

This is why worship is a key to a prophetic life. It is through worship that we are brought into harmonious synchronization with the Father, the Son, and the Holy Spirit. When we come into this fellowship with the Holy Spirit, the mind of Christ, we're taught how to obey. Romans 12 describes another form of worship as "obedience." Those moments when He whispers to our hearts in a still small voice to do something, that is an invitation to worship Him. Our obedience gives us access to a deeper and more meaningful relationship with Jesus and preserves our life. Our lives are saved, hearts restored, bodies healed, minds renewed, and families brought back together when we make it an obligation to obey the Lord.

> **1 Samuel 15:22**
> *Does the LORD delight in burnt offerings and sacrifices as much as in obeying the Lord? To obey is better than sacrifice, and to listen is better than the fat of rams.*

Do you know that worship brings you into revelation? Let's look at the story of Jehosophat.

In 2 Chronicles 20, we see that Jehoshaphat, king of Judah, was facing war against a large army and became afraid. This situation caused him to call a fast and special time of prayer for intervention from the Lord. God encouraged them to stand in their place for the battle they faced wasn't theirs to fight, but it was His. He was brought into this revelation because he chose to bow before the Lord, worship, and pray to Him for intervention. You may at times find yourself during a battle while building a prophetic life, but I urge you to use your key of worship. It will bring you into revelation of the victory that is promised to you through our Lord, Jesus Christ.

Worship unlocks supernatural strategy! Jehosophat and his army did not lift one finger because they stood in the council of the Lord through prayer and worship to receive insight on what they must do. Worship unveils divine mysteries to bring an ambush upon your enemies, just like the armies opposing Judah and Jerusalem. Worship is a powerful key given to believers to receive the answer they need from the Lord.

Be intentional about setting times of worship throughout your day. Starting your day with worship truly helps set your mind and expectations on what God wants to share and/or do through and for you. He truly loves when we set aside uninterrupted time just for him, maybe on our lunch break, or right before we take that phone call with a client.

Worshipping God invites the presence of the Lord right to where you are. Every believer, especially those crafting a prophetic life, need this connection to continually draw strength, love, peace, and joy into their lives. Worship sustains us. Worship brings stability to our heart, mind, and soul by drawing from the well of revelation that is found in the presence of the Lord. Proverbs 14:27 tells us that the fear of the Lord is a fountain of life, by which we may avoid the snares of death. Worship brings us into the fear of the Lord, which is the beginning of wisdom. Worship produces wisdom. Use your prophetic key of worship so that you can craft a stable, holy, and fruitful life through the presence of the Lord.

KEY

4

PRAYER GIVES ACCESS

This prophetic key is one of the foundational elements in the life of every believer of Jesus Christ. Prayer is as a solemn request for help or expression of thanks addressed to God or an object of worship. It is in prayer that we communicate with God through supplication, petitions, thanksgiving, praise, hymns, laments, and entreaty. Prayer establishes intimacy with God, where we take all our cares, concerns, issues, problems, and worries to Him so that He may hear us and respond to our plea.

> **1 Thessalonians 5:17**
> *Pray without ceasing.*

There is no prophetic life without a life of prayer. Prayer helps us to steward and maintain whatever God has given us responsibility for in the Earth. Every major move of God was built on the strength and consistency of prayer. Look at Acts 2 when the day of Pentecost had come as promised. As those gathered were praying, a sound of a rushing mighty wind filled the house where they were sitting.

The introduction and presentation of the Holy Spirit coming into the earth started with prayer. Look at the Azusa Street Revival in 1906 that was birthed from a prayer meeting! Whatever you are believing God for will first be conceived in prayer. You will receive instructions, clarity, insight, and revelation in prayer that will posture you for your next steps.

Prayer is required to access the mind of God concerning your life, family, community, nation, and world. As we communicate with the Holy Spirit through prayer, we share our hearts with Him and He in turn shares the mind of Christ concerning us. The Holy Spirit serves as our mediator in prayer, communicating between us and Jesus, revealing His heart to us in the present. The bible admonishes us to allow Holy Spirit to lead us in prayer.

> ### Romans 8:26
> *In the same way the Spirit comes to us and helps us in our weakness. We do not know what prayer to offer or how to offer it as we should, but the Spirit himself knows our need and at the right time intercedes on our behalf with sighs and groanings too deep for words.*

The Spirit of God, our inner witness, comes and helps us in our weakness by praying through us. Prayer is so important to God that He has given the Holy Spirit charge to help us pray more effectively. It is through prayer that we express our needs, and in faith we stand to receive what we've asked for. Mark 11:24 says that whatsoever you desire, when you pray, believe that you receive them, and you shall have them.

Prayer is a prophetic key because it unlocks every door that's destined for us to enter. We do not have to grow weary or frustrated trying to make things work. Pray about it and watch God make a way.

Prayer brings about solutions to problems and crises. When you look at Acts 12, we see Apostle Peter was bound in chains locked up in prison. The Angel of the Lord appeared to Him and led him out of bondage in Jerusalem. This divine encounter happened while a prayer meeting was taking place at the home of Mary. It surprised the people that were praying when Peter knocked on the door and began to speak to them, because they were praying for him in that very moment. This shows us that while you are communing with the father, your answer can and will show up at your very doorstep. Do not discount or discredit the proactive power of prayer! It is a key that leads to supernatural answers, miracles, and divine intervention in a time of need.

There have been several times in my prophetic journey that I did not initially have a prophetic word for someone, but I felt led to pray for them. While praying for them, God began speaking to me through words of knowledge, symbols, and information about the person's life that led me to prophesy to them.

Prayer is our method of communication to God. We can't find in scripture where it tells us to prophesy daily, but it tells us that we should pray continually without stopping. As followers of Jesus, knowing how to utilize your key of prayer is vital to your spiritual growth. We cannot build a prophetic life without first having a life of prayer.

KEY

5

THE WORD OF GOD

The word of God is single-handedly the most important tool to the life of a believer. The bible tells us that Heaven and Earth shall pass away, but His word will stand forever. It is the literal words of God written by men who were inspired by the Holy Spirit. There is no way that we can build a prophetic life without having a life devoted to the word of God. As believers, we come to know about Jesus through the reading of the word.

When we look at any key to building a prophetic life, the word of God is the foundation by which we experience the supernatural. The bible tells us that man shall not live by bread alone, but by every word that proceeds out of the mouth of God. It is important for us to visualize the word of the Lord as light, not only to recognize it, but to understand it.

> **Psalm 119:130**
> *The entrance of your word brings light; it brings understanding to the simple.*

When the word of God comes into your life, light enters your soul. This light brings full disclosure of what He has planned for you, your family, business, and livelihood. The word of God is full of instruction and discernment, which Ephesians 1:18 describes as having the eyes of your understanding being filled with light. When a person receives the word of God into their soul, transformation happens, hope is renewed, and faith increases.

The word of God makes things visible! It is necessary to access and use what you see in your prophetic life, but it must be prompted by the word of God. If you want to grow in what you see, you will need to increase your study and devotion life. Developing a healthy study life of the word of God will increasingly illuminate your walk, which leads to expanded visibility, clarity, understanding, and wisdom.

> **Psalm 119:105**
> *"Your word is a lamp for my feet, a light for my path!"*

The word of God has the supernatural ability to cast light upon a dark and dismal place and transform it to a meaningful and purposeful place. We will come to points of uncertainty in our lives where we have prayed and asked God for clarity and it seems as if it doesn't exist. We must spend time in devotion consuming the word of God. It will bring us to a place of revelation! We begin to see a path develop, and the place where our feet are currently standing becomes visible from the light shining brightly from the word of God. John 12 describes Jesus as the light that came into the world that men would never have to walk in darkness. John 1 refers to Jesus as the word that became flesh and dwelt among us. Jesus is not only the fulfillment of the Word of God, but he is both the Word and the Light!

Building a prophetic life is impossible without the word of God. All the necessary information you may be looking for about your situation is about to come to you through Jesus, the Word of God. We must come into fellowship with the Word, so it can bring us into this moment of full disclosure. Psalm 84:11 declares that God won't withhold any good thing from you! The word of God brings you into revelation, clarity, understanding, instruction, and discernment. If you want to grow and see increase in your life, build a life as a student of the scriptures so that you can be constantly fed and strengthened by the word of God.

KEY

6

FAITH

Faith is our internal belief system given to us by God. We all experience salvation, redemption, healing, miracles, and even the power of the Scriptures <u>through faith</u>. We come to know the Father, the Son, and the Holy Spirit <u>through faith</u>. Hebrews 11:6 tells us that without faith, it is impossible to please God. Faith is both the key and vehicle by which we navigate through a prophetic life! Faith cultivates our supernatural experience with Jesus through the Holy Spirit.

---

2 Corinthians 5:7
For we walk by faith, not by sight.

The life we live as believers of Jesus Christ never was about walking by what we see, but solely upon what we believe. The bible calls us blessed when we believe and have not seen Jesus. How can this be? FAITH! Faith opens the eyes of our spirit.

Hebrews 11:1
Now faith is the substance (confidence) of things hoped for, and the evidence (assurance) of things not seen.

Faith is the reliance and trust we have in God. This prophetic key gives us the inner confidence to produce outward evidence of things we have not seen. Our entire existence on the Earth is summed up by the faith we have and the love we've shown to one another.

Do you know you make things happen by what you believe?

> **Mark 11:22-23**
> *And Jesus answered them, "Have faith in God. Truly, I say to you, whoever says to this mountain, 'Be taken up and thrown into the sea,' and does not doubt in his heart, but believes that what he says will come to pass, it will be done for him.*

Jesus stressed to the disciples the necessity of having faith in God. Faith doesn't have room for doubt in the heart but only the bold confidence that we place in God. We all know that life presents us with various challenges, but we have been given a divine impartation from God that helps navigate us through each one, our faith.

> **Hebrews 11:3**
> *By faith we understand that the entire universe was formed at God's command, that what we now see did not come from anything that can be seen.*

Faith is a divine currency system that we utilize to make transactions in the spirit. The just shall live by faith! We are those who have been justified by grace through faith by the loving power of Jesus. We literally can call things that are not there to appear by our faith!

> **Romans 12:3**
> *For I say, through the grace given unto me, to every man that is among you, not to think of himself more highly than he ought to think; but to think soberly, according as God hath dealt to every man the measure of faith.*

To fully capture the advantage of this prophetic key, we must use the measure of faith we've been given. God is pleased when we couple our faith in Him with action. Our faith in God produces life, streams of income, health in our soul and body, and brings us into a healthy supernatural life.

It truly takes faith to believe God in the moment to do something that is impossible for men. While you are out grocery shopping, taking a walk in the park, or touring a shopping plaza, the Holy Spirit will call upon your faith to initiate something supernatural. I recall this moment at a gas station that Holy Spirit highlighted this young man to me. I was filling up my car and minding my own business. I did not plan on ministering to anyone at that time.

The Spirit of God began to share with me that this guy was in a dark place and needed prayer. I went over to him and asked if I could pray for him, and he obliged. The faith to initiate this encounter unlocked hidden secrets about this guy. I began to pray against the powers of the enemy that were working against him, as my inner witness led. He began to receive deliverance in the parking lot of a gas station.

With the smell of cigarettes and alcohol on his breath, he hugged me with tears in his eyes. He shared that he was a youth minister who had fell on hard times and lost his way, but that prayer reminded him that God loved him. How many people are waiting for an encounter with God at the expense of you taking a risk on faith?

Your faith in Jesus is your life force. It is your belief system that is directly tied to your actions and output. In other words, what you believe will come out of you! How you believe will be expressed through your actions. You have been given a prophetic key that can bring dead things back to life and resuscitate dreams, visions, and plans that have been abandoned.

KEY

LOVE

Love is such a profound key of a prophetic life. It can be expressed in so many ways from feelings of deep affection to commitment to friendship and selflessness. Showing love to others is how we are marked as disciples of Jesus. Love is transformative. My testimony is that my life would not have been changed had I not first encountered the love of Jesus. His love captivated me, transformed me from a sinner to a son of God. I am forever grateful for his unwavering love that He shows towards me.

> ### John 3:16
> *For God so loved the world that He gave his only begotten Son, that whosoever believes in him should not perish, but have everlasting life.*

We have received salvation as one of the greatest acts of love ever been given to humanity. Jesus tells us in John 15:13, "Greater love hath no man than this, that a man lay down his life for his friends." Jesus laid down his life for us because he loved us, and through this act of love he reconciled us back to the family of God.

A beautiful revelation that scripture unveils about love is that it is the door to the supernatural. New covenant believers have a standard now by which we are to walk and live by. Love and compassion must be the basis by which we minister to others so that we are effective.

> ## 1 Corinthians 13:1-3
> *If I speak in the tongues of men or of angels, but do not have love, I am only a resounding gong or a clanging cymbal. If I have the gift of prophecy and can fathom all mysteries and all knowledge, and if I have a faith that can move mountains, but do not have love, I am nothing. If I give all I possess to the poor and give over my body to hardship that I may boast, but do not have love, I gain nothing.*

What benefit do we have to live a life prophesying, working wonders, performing miracles, healing the sick, raising the dead, making disciples in the nations of the earth, and funding kingdom initiatives across the globe if we do not walk in love? We gain nothing from any of it. The only guaranteed way that any of what He has given us will count is if it is done in love and charity.

A prophetic life is a life that is madly in love with Jesus. For our relationship with Jesus to fully be expressed, we must love who He loves. He loves all of humanity, those who love him and those who don't.

> ## 1 Corinthians 13: 8
> *Love never fails. But whether there are prophecies, they will fail; whether there are tongues, they will cease; whether there is knowledge, it will vanish away.*

Love is the greatest commandment given by Jesus. This is critical for prophetic people to understand and apply. When we perfect how we love, we become more like God. Although love is the last key I discussed in this book, it is the greatest commandment according to scripture. We would not know Jesus had it not been for the love of God! There are many dismal places we would have been had it not been for the love of God pursuing us.

A prophetic life is a life led by love. As we grow to view humanity through the eyes of love, we see in them what God intends and wills for them. Observing creation through love brings us into the Father's heart for it and allows us to experience just a piece of the overwhelming compassion He has for His creation. This is the place we are to build our prophetic life from. This is the lens by which we are to prophesy, work miracles, pray for healing, and raise the dead. Your journey to cultivating a prophetic life will be more vivid because of the love you walk in.

FINAL REMARKS

It is my hope that this body of work has blessed you. My desire is to please God and to help others build a healthy prophetic life that the Lord will honor. Prophecy isn't the total experience or reward for the believer, but it is how we posture ourselves to see Jesus in every area of our lives that counts. Knowing Jesus through the Holy Spirit is the greatest joy of our lives. Take these 7 keys and apply them to your everyday routine, and I guarantee you that you will experience God in a brand-new way.

LET ME PRAY OVER YOU:

Father, I come in the name of Jesus thanking you for the opportunity to love and be loved by you. I thank you for your son that you gave to the world as a gift because of your great love. I am grateful that you have given us the precious gift of the Holy Spirit, who testifies to us of Jesus, just as Jesus testifies of you. I thank you that you have equipped us through your word to be effective witnesses of you in the Earth. I pray that the revelation you have developed in my life, and which you have given me clearance to share with others, strengthens their faith. I pray that you would begin to impart new technology, administrations, and expressions of the Holy Spirit within them as they journey in building a prophetic life that hon-

7 Keys for a Prophetic Life

ors you. May everything they do be in love and may it last. I thank you, my God, that you are aligning their footsteps now to your will. May you give them every place the sole of their feet tread upon. Remind them of their authority in the spirit realm through Jesus Christ, our Lord. May they advance to new heights, territories, and realms as they grow in a healthy relationship with the word of God. May they find a community of believers who will nurture, water, and build the prophetic on the inside of them.

I bind the spirit of fear, anxiety, isolation, and every lie that would be uttered from hell against these your people. I declare that they will come into community, form healthy relationships, and fulfill the purpose of the Lord as written in Ephesians 4. Your son, your daughter, will perfect the saints, do the work of ministry, and bring edification to the body of Christ in all that they do.

I prophesy that they will prosper and be in good health, even as their souls prosper. I declare that their cupboards will never run empty, and that whatsoever they do will prosper. I declare Psalm 1 over them, that as they make the word of God a delight in their hearts, that you will make them as trees planted by the rivers of water which flourishes in every season. Thank you that the blood of Jesus covers their family, friends, job, investments, and everything connected to them.

May you pour out your spirit upon them as your word declared it would in Joel 2:28. May your sons and daughters prophesy, old men dream dreams, young men see visions, and may the same spirit fall upon the servants and handmaids. Fill us until we overflow, Father. May we never lose our desire for more of you. May we always have a heart desperately wanting you, Jesus. Bless the reader in a special way. May their lives be marked by prophetic happenings, and never let them be the same from this day forward. AMEN.

PHILLIP BRYANT

PHILLIP BRYANT MINISTRIES

Phillip Bryant is a passionate man of faith with a driving force to help people discover their identity and purpose. With over 15 years of experience as a worship leader, speaker, and intercessor, Phillip is on a mission to provide a community where discipleship and transformation happens through God's truth and love. Phillip is a certified life coach and mentor who is driven to help others discover their identity and walk in their purpose. Phillip is the loving husband to Hope Bryant and knows that we all are born to have a significant impact on the world.

www.ingramcontent.com/pod-product-compliance
Lightning Source LLC
Chambersburg PA
CBHW041811040426
42449CB00004B/145